Published by The Kwak Brothers

Thekwakbrothers.com

Table of Contents

Disclaimer & Disclosure

The authors and the distributors of this book do not warrant, promise, and/or guarantee any specific results, outcomes, profit, earnings, and/or income. Readers are advised to always consult with licensed professionals before engaging in any financial strategies or business transactions. This book does not offer any investments nor does it offer any tax, legal, or financial advice. This book is written with an educational purpose only. Readers and those that have this book in their possession are solely responsible for the outcomes, results, or the lack thereof when using the strategies, tactics, and ideas represented in this book.

Introduction

Congratulations! Why? Because you're part of a very small group of people who actually want to change your financial ecosystem. Instead of accepting the status quo or surrendering to the mediocre path, you have chosen to learn and improve your finances.

We applaud you for that!

So let's not waste time with a boring introduction.

What? You thought that this book was going to be boring?

Well, let me paint a picture of what's possible. Here is Cristy. She's a client of ours who is using the very information we're going to share with you in this book.

She used our strategy to pay down $41,000 of her mortgage balance in just four months.

Feeling bored yet?

How about this one?

Now, ready for something shocking?

Both of these clients were able to achieve this without having to:

1. Send in extra payments out of their pocket to the existing mortgage.
2. Refinance into another mortgage
3. Modify their mortgage.
4. Hurt their credit.
5. Win a lottery.

So, how did they do it? What was the “trick”? Is this magic?

Well, it’s certainly not magic but it does involve some math – the kind of math that saves you money and time!

The best part about all this is that both of these clients are well on their way to paying off their mortgages but they can also use this same strategy as a springboard to real estate investing, buying businesses, or even creating a healthy retirement.

At the end of the day, it’s all about setting you free so that you can retire early, build a legacy, and have more options in life. No one wants to be stuck in a mortgage or continue working past their retirement age, right?

Ch 1. What's So Bad about Your Mortgage?

At the time of this book, the 30-year mortgage interest rate is at a historically low point. Plus, there are talks of hyper-inflation which tends to make low interest loans favorable. So when we share this idea of using the Accelerated Banking Strategy to pay off mortgages faster, many of our critics say,

"Why would you pay off your mortgage when interest rates are so stinkin' low?!"

We would, of course, agree that the interest rates are really low right now! And that's great! But what most bankers and mortgage professionals don't talk about is the fact that A LOT of other variables have changed in the home lending world.

In the late 1970s and throughout the 1980s, the typical mortgage interest rates were around 12-16%. Some were higher. You could have also deposited your money in a savings account and earned 10-12% -- sometimes even higher. What a crazy time in our financial history!

But what most people *don't* talk about is the fact that prior to the 1990s, a large amount of mortgages was on 5-, 10- or even 15-year amortization at most.

The whole idea of a 30-year mortgage is quite new.

When the interest rates were really high, most people were on 5- to 15-year amortizations to offset the fact that they would pay a large amount of interest if they prolonged the pay-off.

But with the 30-year amortization being the norm these days, individuals don't realize that they're paying a considerable amount of interest throughout the 30-year period even with a lower interest rate.

Not to mention, with the introduction of government-backed programs such as Freddie Mac and Fannie Mae, the 30-year amortization mortgage has become the "normal".

And what's more interesting is that the lifestyle of the average person has changed.

Long gone are the days when you could settle for the same house with your same job for 20-40 years and expect a perfect retirement.

Those days don't exist anymore.

The economic and financial landscape has changed, and the average person moves quite often.

It is estimated that today the average American moves 11.7 times in their lifetime.(2) This could be due to new job opportunities, political changes, moving out of the state to avoid taxes, or even life-events such as downsizing. Let's assume that most people live 80-100 years. That means that the average person moves every 7-10 years. I'll explain why this fact is so important pretty soon.

Now, let's talk about *WHY* you need to pay off your mortgage faster. Yes, the interest rates are historically low. And yes, you could be investing your dollars elsewhere. But here's the groundbreaking reason as to why doing NOTHING about your mortgage will keep you perpetually stuck in your mortgage and never accumulating wealth.

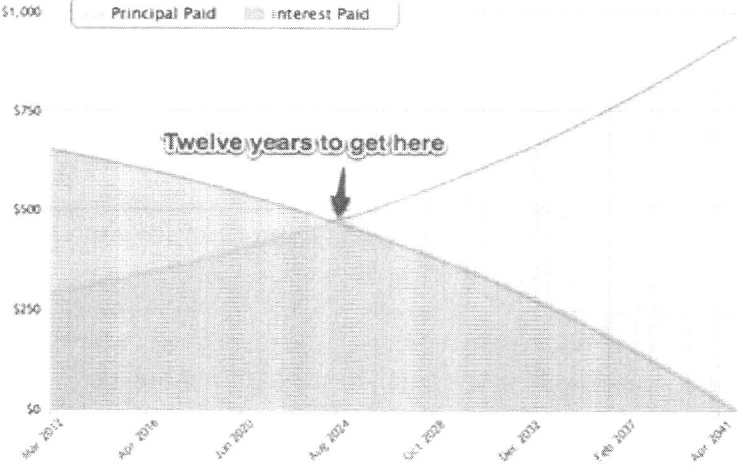

Above is an amortization chart. All mortgages, student loans, and even auto-loans run on an amortized calculation. A little fun fact about the word "amortization" is that the prefix "a" is often used to describe something that is "not" or "without". The word "mort" comes from the French word that means "death". So when you combine these two meanings together, you can say that it means "to not die". In other words, an amortized loan is a loan that **never dies**. Some lending professionals would disagree with this interpretation of the word but that is the truth behind it.

On the chart, the line that goes from left to right represents the amount of time you spend in paying down the mortgage. The line that is vertical (up and down) represents the monthly mortgage payment amount.

If you notice on the chart, the yellow highlighted area represents the amount of interest you pay in proportion to your monthly mortgage payment. You notice that the yellow highlighted area is at its biggest in the very beginning of the chart on the left. That means, the vast majority of the interest is paid upfront.

So if you just recently started on your mortgage payments or you refinanced, a large portion of your early payments are actually going to the interest and not to lowering the loan's balance.

As time goes on, more and more of your monthly payment does go to the principal balance which is represented by the blue highlighted area in the chart. Principal is the actual balance of the mortgage. The more principal we pay down, the better it is for us.

But just as the chart indicates, it takes 12 years to get to a point where there's a crossing-over to where more of your monthly payment goes towards the principal. Now, this is just an example figure. Your mortgage may have a faster or a slower crossing-over point. So please note that it's not always 12 years. It can be 8, 10, 12, or even 15 years depending on the interest rate.

Now here's where the BIG problem is.

It doesn't matter whether you have a low interest rate or that you have a lower payment than others. There are two major problems that most homeowners don't think about.

The First BIG Problem With Your Mortgage

Remember how We mentioned the fact that the average American moves every 7-10 years? Here's how that fits in.

Let's say you made it to the 7–10-year mark in paying down your mortgage. You've been a homeowner for nearly a decade. Great work!

But once you decide you want to sell your house, move to a new home, and get a brand new 30-year mortgage – do you get to continue your progress on your previous mortgage? Meaning, can you pick back up from where you were on the amortization chart?

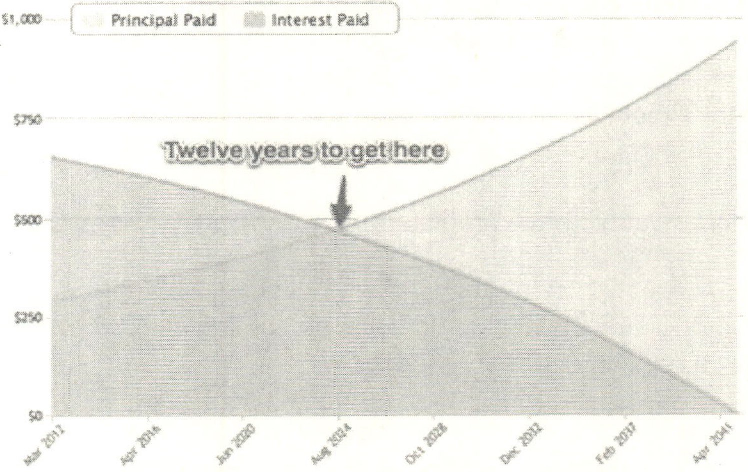

The answer is 'no'. The moment you get a brand new 30-year mortgage on your new home, you have to start all over again where the vast majority of your monthly mortgage payment goes straight to interest.

Sure, you also made a bit of a contribution to the mortgage paydown but it's not enough.

Looking at the chart again, moving before the 12-year mark to start over would simply mean that you never had the opportunity to make a significant impact on your principal balance reduction.

Ouch...

Let alone, if the statistic is true, then you would expect to repeat that process once again in 7-10 years.

You may make the case and say *"Well, I'm never going to move. I'm going to stick around for a very long time."* But the problem is that none of us has a magical crystal ball to make that kind of a commitment when the world is changing so fast.

No one could have predicted the COVID-19 pandemic in 2020-2021.

No one saw the economic collapse coming in 2008 except for a handful of observant people.

Therefore, you can't guarantee that you'll stick around long enough to where you can make it beyond the 15-year mark on your amortization schedule.

So even with a lower interest rate, the 30-year amortization combined with the fact that most people move every 7-10 years, makes it vital that homeowners focus on paying off their mortgage faster, especially in ever-changing economic times.

The Second Problem With Your Mortgage

Now, let's say this is a perfect world and you know for a fact that you won't move in the next 20-30 years.

That's great!

But here's the other problem.

Every now and then, you'll get an advertising piece in the mail, or you see a promotion on the internet of an extremely low interest rate. Occasionally, you may get a mortgage broker or a banker that reaches out to you with an offer to lower your mortgage payment.

Unfortunately, this is where most people get duped.

Some homeowners hear that "lower monthly payment" offer as some kind of way to save money. But what mortgage brokers do is nothing different than most car sales reps. They focus on the monthly payment.

Car salesmen or women know that as long as you focus on the monthly payment and not the actual price of the car, they win. Why? Because they know that by offering you a lower monthly payment, they can prolong the interest amount they can earn and/or they can increase the price on the car which means more commission for them.

The same logic applies to your mortgage. Mortgage brokers know that they can get you to focus on the monthly payment amount but not the actual interest you pay over time.

I'm not saying that all mortgage professionals and car sales reps are evil. Some of them don't even know that this is the case.

But it doesn't relieve you of the responsibility you have to protect your finances.

So, what mortgage brokers do is convince you to refinance to a lower monthly payment. And by refinancing into another 30-year mortgage, you're essentially starting all over, where the vast majority of your monthly payment is going towards the interest.

Now there are some cases where refinancing does make sense. Especially for homeowners who financed their home using high-interest hard money loans. But these cases are rare.

Imagine refinancing every 7-10 years into a brand new 30-year mortgage – never getting to any significant principal reduction. Technically, the bank owns more of the home than you do.

You might as well have been renting all those years, where you paid for repairs, renovations, and maintenance. But you're again facing 20-30 years to go on your mortgage whenever you refinance at any moment of your homeownership.

So, if you've been expecting to pay off your mortgage and earn a nice retirement – don't be surprised by the fact that you still have 20+ years to go.

Feeling upset yet?

But It's Not Your Fault…

So, here's the thing, it's not your fault that you didn't know about this. In fact, We believe it's purposely designed this way to keep all of us in the dark.

Our education system doesn't teach us about investing, managing our finances, how the tax system works, and how banking works.

Think about it... We spend our first 18 years of life learning everything else *but* money. Somehow, calculus has become more important than learning how to create value in the marketplace.

If more people understood how banking works and how our tax systems are set up, we think more people would figure out how to pay less interest, less taxes, and how to thrive economically.

We believe that if more people became financially literate, it could certainly trickle down to solving all kinds of real-world problems like homelessness and poverty.

Heck! It might even solve marital issues as one of the top five reasons for divorce has to do with money(1).

But we also believe that once you've been made aware of this, it becomes up to you to pursue financial literacy and freedom. It is now your responsibility to take the information we're sharing and actually do something about it.

"But I just want to stick with the traditional method and wait 30 years to be done with my mortgage!"

Let's say you have a starting mortgage balance of $250,000 (a little above the national average) at 5% interest and 30-year amortization loan.

I'm going to calculate the interest for you using THIS calculator found online: https://www.amortization-calc.com/

If you steadily paid the mortgage down for the entire 30 years, you would have paid $233,139 in JUST interest alone.

So, if you combine the actual loan balance of $250,000 with the interest you're paying, you are going to end up paying a grand total of $483,139! THAT'S MONEY OUT OF YOUR POCKET! WHAT?!

Some of you might be saying, "Well, but that's how things are..."

No, it's not...

It wasn't always like this until the last 30 years when the banks started to introduce the idea of the 30-year amortization.

Just take a look at this... (United States)

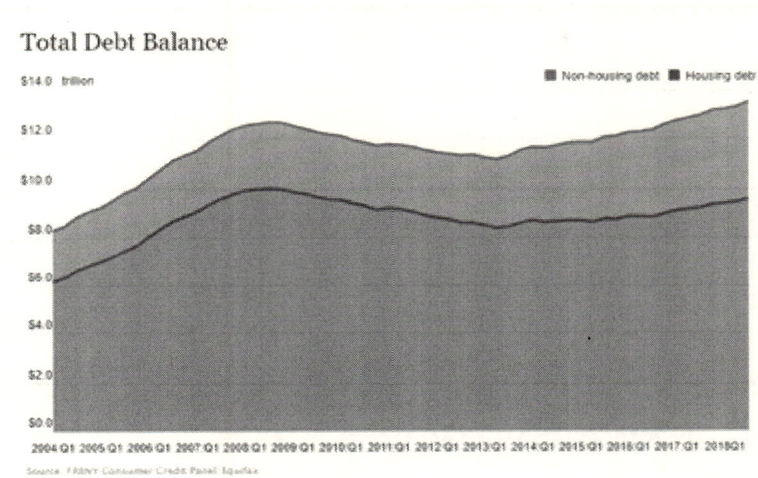

Do you notice how we have MORE consumer debt now than ever? Mind you, the most recent data this graph shows is 2018. The trend for this graph is showing that we are on a rise to more debt.

This is NOT looking good.

Remember how we talked about the amount of interest you would be paying on a 30-year mortgage? Well look at all those people with ever more debt... Looks like the real winners here are the banks!

So why not keep as much money as possible and invest that into an income-producing asset, like real estate? Keep more of the money you make and take control of it. That's the name of the game!

So, this is why your mortgage is dangerous.

You're stuck!

The banks got you where they want you to be.

Ignorant and trapped...

This system only feeds the banks more money.

Luckily, there's another way! A NEW Opportunity!

Introducing the Accelerated Banking Strategy

The Accelerated Banking Strategy is all about cash flow management. And we believe that the foundation of everyone's financial future is and should be cash flow management.

Again, this is not taught in the schools or even in most college finance courses. This must be first -- the number one -- financial priority. Everything else then stacks or layers on top to be able to manage and invest the cash flow and cash assets to create new income streams and build wealth.

This is about interest-avoidance not changing your lifestyle or sacrificing! It's simply about taking control of your cash flow by no longer giving free loans to the banks. It's your money and you, not the banks, deserve the daily benefit of your money.

To me a bank is only useful when We need to borrow money to create new income. What We mean by this is there is good debt and bad debt. Debt equals interest-payments-are-due, so good interest and bad interest.

Bad debt equals paying interest for a place to live, to drive a car, to buy something on a credit card and pay interest for a dinner you ate last year or a vacation you took 3 years ago. So many people are paying bad interest each and every day. These are the dollars we have to stop wasting on interest by implementing advanced cash flow strategies.

Good interest is using the bank to finance a rental property or vacation home that creates a new income stream. Using an equity line to flip a home for profit, or to become the bank and use arbitrage to loan money at a higher rate than you are paying. For example, borrow at 4% and loan at 7% or more.

There are many opportunities for the income generated where borrowing exceeds the amount of interest due creating positive cash flow. The interest becomes a justifiable business expense because the income stream would not be possible without borrowing from the bank.

Again, we use the bank and the loan as our tools to increase our income and wealth, instead of the bank using the loan as a tool to extract wealth from us. It's actually a win-win as we gain income streams and wealth, and the bank earns interest income. If it's not a win-win we don't do it. It's that simple.

We all know that the banks are scared of a run on the bank where we want our money back because they've lent out more than we deposited. They can't give it all back at once.

But they are equally terrified of an interruption of their cash flow. Without new daily deposits, their cash flow, they are doomed.

Imagine if people got together and decided the bank had lost their trust and quit depositing new funds or if payroll auto-deposits were stopped. The banks would panic. Cash flow is their power, and the average person doesn't even realize it.

With our strategy, we don't give the banks free loans by using their traditional checking and savings accounts. Instead, we use the tools they provide such as HELOCs, PLOCs and BLOCs to manage our cash flow. We use the banks' services and will pay them for that service, but not a penny more.

If we borrow money, we will pay the daily interest, but we know when we put our head on the pillow each night we know that we are paying the absolute least amount possible. No more free loans to the bank.

Ch 2. Origin Story

Sam Kwak

For those that don't know who I am, my name is Sam Kwak. My brother, Daniel, and I have been investing in real estate since when we were 23 and 21 years old, respectively. Now we teach real estate, and we manage a hedge fund that invests in large commercial real estate projects.

At the time of this book, I'm 28 and Daniel is 26.

We began our journey into the financial and real estate business when we were still back in college.

To go back even further, my brother and I immigrated to the United States from South Korea with my parents in 1999 – or I should say that my parents immigrated here and we just happened to be part of that decision. Our father is a church pastor who was asked to take over a Korean-American church in Chicago.

Scared, afraid and alone, our family came to the United States with no more than $2000 in cash, speaking little-to-no English or comprehension, and little-to-no network to ask for help.

We moved into a small 1-bedroom apartment, about 800 square feet. We were a family of four crammed into a tiny apartment. I remember my parents had their bed set up in the dining area next to the kitchen. My brother and I slept on the floor in the bedroom.

I also remember one time our family couldn't even pay the bills in the middle of Chicago's January. If you've ever been to Chicago in January, the temperatures can easily drop below into the negatives. Without heat, our family had to sleep in our family van while the engine was running to keep us warm.

To make things even more “real”, I remember our mom went out to our local park and picked dandelion leaves so she could make salad (which by the way, it’s healthy for you!) That’s how poor we were when we first came to America.

I also remember our family having to face near-deportation from the United States because our immigration attorney didn’t properly follow the procedures of applying for a permanent residency status. Ultimately, our visa expired, and we were due for deportation.

We ended up going to court and through God’s blessing and grace, the judge granted us a path to citizenship, and we ended up staying here in this country. This was 2008 when the economy was falling apart.

We grew up with this “poor” mentality that the only way to live in the U.S. was to get into debt, go get a job, and work for 40 years to retire on a fraction of the income that you were used to.

As we grew into our college years, we realized that we had to make a decision. We were at a fork in the road: choose the status quo (working for a job, getting in debt, retiring late) OR choose to challenge the status quo by doing what the 99% of the people aren’t doing.

We came across a book called *Rich Dad Poor Dad* that changed EVERYTHING for us. We were introduced to this concept of real estate investing which also opened the door of financial literacy.

We realized that if we could buy houses where people would pay us rent to live, we wouldn't have to "slave away" at a corporate job for the rest of our lives. If we just got enough people paying us rent, we knew we would become financially free.

I remember feeling excited by this new "enlightenment" that I had. I just had this rush of wanting to take action and start buying properties.

But we had a problem.

I had neither the money nor the credit to start buying houses.

I felt stuck, frustrated, and annoyed by the fact that things weren't moving fast enough for me.

We began exploring ways to invest in real estate. We took courses, attended seminars, listened to podcasts, and spent whatever money we had (very little) in learning as much as we could.

After a long journey of searching, we finally found a mentor who took us under his wing and taught us everything he knew, and in one particular year, my brother and I bought over 75 rental units!

As I've mentioned, my brother and I now invest primarily through our own hedge fund company. We still have our own private portfolio of apartments. We also enjoy investing and buying businesses along the side.

In one of the seminars we attended in our early days, we came across this one little "secret" strategy. It's called the Accelerated Banking Strategy. Chances are, you bought this book because you want to get familiar with this strategy and apply it to your situation.

Before our real estate successes, I remember having a critical moment in my life. I was still back in college. I walked out of my apartment to check for mail. It was a normal day and nothing special was going on other than the smell of pizza that the other college kids ordered.

I opened my mailbox and stacks of envelopes had come. Curious, I started walking back to my apartment while examining the mail that I was holding.

I opened them. One by one. I can still remember the crisp sound of the envelopes being torn open.

As I opened the folded pieces of paper, I remember this sick feeling in my stomach that came as I read through the pieces of paper.

They were my credit card statements.

This sick feeling in my stomach became a silent panic. It was almost as if I was screaming in my head.

At that moment, I realized that my debt had spun out of control. I was only in college and yet I was getting buried in debt. Credit cards, student loans, and getting more credit cards. I was barely making money DJ-ing for weddings and birthday parties.

My minimum payments started to go up and I knew I couldn't handle them. I had to figure it out...

No more partying. No more hiding or pretending that the debt wasn't there. I had to take responsibility for my actions.

Thankfully, through hard work in real estate investing and building up my businesses - things became easier. Especially when I started to implement the Accelerated Banking Strategy.

My debt started to wither away. One by one... One credit card after another.

It WORKED! I couldn't believe it!!!

I started to realize 'Wait, if this worked for me... How many people out there could benefit from this too?!'

Later, I created a YouTube video titled "How to Pay off Your Mortgage in 5-7 Years" and decided to upload it. At the time, I was honestly wanting to share how cool this strategy was. I wasn't necessarily looking for subscribers or fame. I just wanted to share it with everyone.

Little did I know, this one video would change THOUSANDS of homeowners' lives.

One individual is Denice.

Denice
October 12 at 4:50 PM

Thought you might like an update. We started in June so it has been about 4 months. I figured out that we have paid down 12% on our mortgage and that has advanced us three and a half years towards our payoff. The interest on the HELOC has only been about $30 and the rewards on our Citi double cash credit card have been over $100. So the rewards on the card are more than covering the interest on the HELOC. We have been living on our usual budget and have even had two significant car repairs in the process. I am pleased with the results.

Denice is one of my clients who used the Accelerated Banking Strategy to pay down her mortgage. In her first four months of using this strategy, she paid down 12% of her mortgage and skipped 3.5 years on her mortgage schedule.

Remember the amortization chart we referenced earlier in chapter 1? Basically, she skipped 3.5 years closer to the "principal pay-down zone."

That's not all! I taught her about another concept called the "Hybrid Method". The Hybrid Method involves using a credit card to handle all purchases thus earning points while you simultaneously avoid paying the interest using our strategy! (More on this later)

Using her credit cards, she earned over $100 worth of cash-back. She essentially got paid to use our strategy! Sweet! That's not all. Denice sent me her 6-month results:

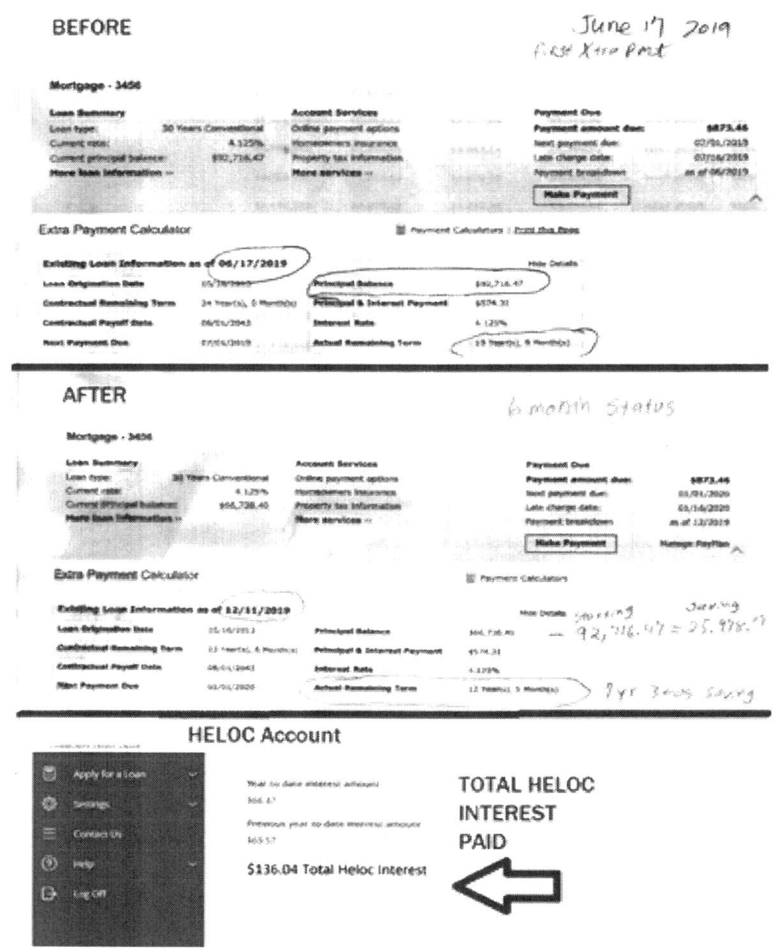

Denice's Mortgage Statement Comparison

If you notice, she sent me the mortgage statement for June 2019. Six months after using our strategy, she sent me another mortgage statement issued December 2019.

During those six months, her mortgage balance went down from $92,716.47 to $66,736.40. That's $25,978.07 of her principal balance that was shaved off! (Wow!)

Even better, she went from having 19 years and 8 months on her mortgage to 12 years and 5 months. Which means that she saved 7 years and 3 months.

All that in six months!

Remember, this is without having to refinance, send extra payments to the existing mortgage, modifying the mortgage, or hurting her credit.

You'll quickly find out that this strategy also gives you MORE freedom and flexibility.

Seeing stories like Denice's, I began my journey to help others find the same solution and help I did. I want to help transform YOU to become free from your mortgage. My transformation wasn't just about getting rid of my debt. It was an epiphany that other people needed this too.

My mission now is to help people grasp this concept and even more -- help them build an empire where they don't HAVE to work for the rest of their lives; instead, create a source of passive income so that they can spend more time with family, connect with more people, travel more, experience life and provide for those that they love!

Whether you have a large mortgage, auto loan, student loan or credit cards, this strategy is the PERFECT way to pay off your debt to live free!

Now that you know what's possible , let's get into how the strategy works. we know you have questions and concerns.

When we first found out about this strategy, we wondered 'How could this strategy work when the interest rate on the line of credit is HIGHER than the mortgage?!' OR 'The math just doesn't make sense... How does the strategy work?!'. Chances are, you have questions right now like we did when we first came across this strategy.

The good news is...

We have the answers!

David Bruce

My name is David Bruce and I have been in the mortgage industry for over 28 years and owned four mortgage companies during my career.

Over the past five years I have personally used the Accelerated Banking Strategy for my family, paying off our house in 13 months, and helped over 1000 families across the U.S. get started using the Accelerated Banking Strategy.

I was first introduced to the strategy in 2006 when a bank from Australia brought the program to the United States. I was so excited as I knew it would change the entire mortgage industry. But before it could really catch on, the market crashed.

The Australian bank went home and the strategy never got traction here in the United States. It wasn't until 2015 that I learned the strategy never really went away but was sitting on a shelf at the banks and no one was really talking about it.

It's like a bank secret they don't want you to know! It was on the shelf as a 1st lien HELOC and I never realized it was available the entire time.

As you can imagine, as an owner of a mortgage company at the time, I was livid that I didn't know it was available. After all, if I didn't know as an industry insider, what's the chance that the general public could learn this bank secret?

For months, I truly couldn't forgive myself for not knowing until finally one day my wife told me to just shut up and get over it. She said we are already using the strategy for our family and you are helping other families get started, so the past is the past and just focus on the future of helping more families do what we are doing.

I realized that she was right and I decided right then that I would dedicate the remainder of my career to helping families implement the Accelerated Banking Strategy.

My mission now is to help as many families as possible, as early in their financial life cycle as possible, to learn the banking secrets and stop being taken advantage of by the banks. I want families to educate themselves so they have a chance to get ahead financially and focus on creating generational wealth.

My goal is to change lives one HELOC at a time! You may be thinking... 'So what's so special about a HELOC and this strategy that can change your life?' It's really pretty simple.

A HELOC (home equity line of credit) is the tool that allows you to take control of your cash flow management so you can pay less interest! Less interest means more money goes to principal faster which leads to lower interest expenses for you and a faster payoff.

The earlier you learn that cash flow management is priority #1, the sooner you can adjust so that you can accomplish other important financial goals.

If you are young and haven't bought your first home yet, I want to help you buy a home with this strategy and avoid the mortgage death pledge.

If you already own a home and have a mortgage, I want to teach you cash flow management strategies to pay off your balance faster and pay less interest so your hard-earned money can be reinvested to accomplish other financial goals such as creating new income streams thru real estate investment, saving for you children's education, saving for retirement, and creating generational wealth through real estate investing and the infinite banking concept (discussed in later chapter).

Not managing cash flow properly can be the #1 reason that keeps you from accomplishing these goals. If you have kids, interest savings can help fund their education. If you are short on retirement funds, interest savings can help you catch up on your retirement goals.

Think of The Kwak Brothers as leaders of a community of like-minded families using advanced cash flow strategies like Accelerated Banking Strategy.

Everyone shares a common set of core values to manage their finances. Combining strategies to minimize and avoid paying unnecessary interest, to quickly reduce debt, to manage home equity and leverage it to acquire income producing assets, to protect those assets on a path to debt-free home ownership and to creating generational wealth.

I say HELOC also stands for:

H helping

E everyone

L leverage

O our

C cashflow

HELOC = Liquidity!

Liquidity = Peace of Mind!

Liquidity = Opportunity!

Access to home equity is vitally important. It's better to have access and not use it than need access and not have it available.

Ch 3. The Strategy…

All right, so you understand why your mortgage can be so dangerous so we need a new vehicle to start paying off your mortgage. Right now, your 30-year mortgage is like a horse. And this strategy is kind of like a brand-new Corvette.

Photo Courtesy of Pexels & Pixabay

Both a horse and a Corvette can help you get to your destination. But the Corvette is a lot faster (and fun too!).

So where DID this strategy come from? How did it start?

Well, no one knows the true origins but the use of the strategy by ordinary individuals started in Australia and New Zealand. In fact, a good number of the population in

Australia use this strategy to pay down their mortgages. It's actually quite mainstream!

It is rumored that the strategy made its way to the United States in the early 2000s and homeowners started to use it.

In Australia, they use something called an "offset account". Unfortunately, here in the U.S. and Canada, we don't have an offset account. But what we do have is a line of credit that we can use to make the strategy work.

There are different types of lines of credit:

- Home Equity Line of Credit (HELOC)
- Personal Line of Credit (PLOC)
- Business Line of Credit (BLOC)
- Commercial Line of Credit***
- Share Stock Secured Line of Credit (SSLOC)
- Secured Line of Credit (SLOC)
- Cryptocurrency Line of Credit
- Checking Line of Credit

HELOC - Home Equity Line of Credit

This is the most popular method if you're dealing with a mortgage. If all you have is your student loan or your auto loan, a HELOC will not work for you because it is a line of credit that uses your equity in your home as a collateral. It's kind of like your home becoming a bank.

Once you get a HELOC, whatever money you have paid into paying off your mortgage can now be drawn back out as long as it fits inside the Loan-To-Value percentage.

The Loan-To-Value (LTV) is expressed in a percentage form and it has to do with how much you can borrow related to the amount of equity you have or the value of your home.

For example, let's say you have a $100,000 house and you don't owe anything on it. You go to the bank and they are offering you a 90% LTV loan which means they are willing to lend you $90,000. If you have an existing mortgage of say $60,000, the bank will only give you another $30,000. Does that make sense?

Most HELOCs are within the 80-90% LTV range. Some banks may require you to be at 65-75% LTV.

BLOC - Business Line of Credit

A BLOC is best if you are either self-employed or you have a business. Business owners don't get paid as employees do, so sometimes it may be hard to prove your income. That's where a BLOC comes in handy.

It is an unsecured line of credit meaning that there is no collateral attached to the line of credit. You may see a high interest rate since it's unsecured but it's not significantly higher.

Usually, most banks will offer a BLOC without any verification of income if you need less than a $100,000 limit. This is great for self-employed individuals.

There are issues with co-mingling funds but there are ways around it so that you're doing things legally and ethically.

PLOC - Personal Line of Credit

A PLOC is better suited if you are paying off your student loans or auto loans. This is the next best thing to a HELOC. Typically, you' l get a smaller limit with a PLOC. The highest I've personally seen is a $20,000 limit. That's because most PLOCs are used for personal items and, unlike businesses, people usually spend on frivolous things.

The PLOC qualification process is similar to that of a BLOC minus the need for a business. You do need to have a certain credit score, and verification of income may be needed to prove that you can pay it back.

LOC vs. A Mortgage

So what *is* the difference between a line of credit and a mortgage? Sure, they're both instruments for debt. But they have stark differences.

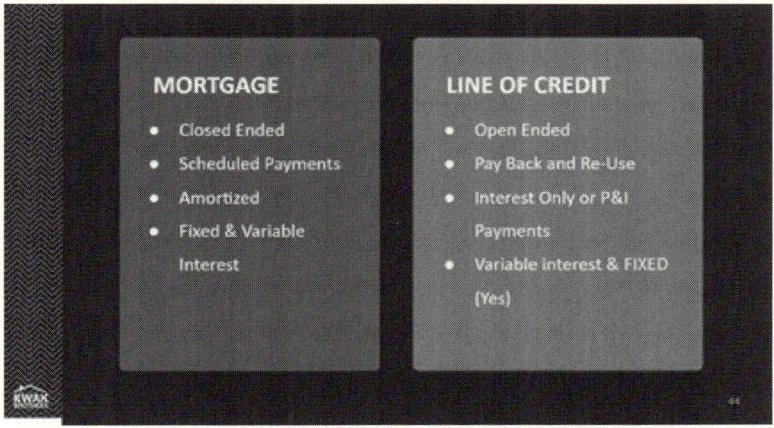

First thing first, a mortgage is closed ended. That means that your monthly mortgage payment is used to pay down the mortgage but you can't ever take any money back out of the mortgage whenever you want.

Whereas with the line of credit, you can use, pay back, and re-use the money on it. If that sounds familiar, your credit card is a form of a line of credit.

However, unlike a credit card, a true line of credit allows you to convert your available limit into cash without paying a "cash advance fee". With a true line of credit, converting it into ready and available cash is incredibly easy.

It's extremely liquid – meaning conversion to cash is fast and easy. In fact, it takes a couple of seconds in most cases.

Access to equity is vitally important. Access could mean opportunity! Would you buy a safe and put all your money in it and throw away the key? No, you want to be able to open the safe and get your money when you need it.

A line of credit is the safe that gives you access to your equity. Think of the line of credit as a parking lot. It's where you should park your savings instead of depositing it into a checking or savings account and letting it sit with a 0% yield.

You can "park" your savings in the line of credit until it is needed. This gives you the benefit of lowering your daily balance and changing the way interest is calculated down to the daily level. We'll talk more about this later.

A mortgage interest rate can be fixed or be variable. One of the big myths we often have to bust is that "all lines of credit interest rates are variable".

This is simply not true.

There are lines of credit that come with fixed interest rates. Depending on the type of a line of credit, you may even find interest rates as low as 2-3%. And yes, even at a fixed rate!

Another stark contrast is how the interest is calculated on a mortgage versus the line of credit using our strategy.

We will preface this by saying that both a mortgage and a line of credit is calculated using a daily balance. From the surface, you can't really tell the difference between how the mortgage and line of credit interests are calculated.

But if you take a closer look, you will understand why the line of credit has a distinct advantage over the mortgage. Here is why.

Let's say your monthly income is $7500. In your effort to pay down the mortgage, let's say you put the entire $7,500 of your monthly income towards your mortgage.

You might be saying, *"What?! Why would I do that?! How am I going to have the funds to pay for my other bills and expenses?!"* Because the moment you make a principal payment on your mortgage, you cannot reuse those funds.

But with the line of credit, however, you could take your entire income amount and make a principal payment against the line of credit balance.

And remember how you can withdraw funds out of the line of credit at any time? That line of credit will also give you the ability to pay for your expenses and bills later.

So let's talk about this term "daily interest".

It's REALLY important for you to understand how the interest is calculated because without it, you'll struggle to understand the "*why*" part of how this strategy works.

LOC Average Daily Interest Calculation

Average Daily Balance (ADB) and Average Daily Interest (ADI) is the math behind how loans are charged with interest.

Daily Balance & DAILY INTEREST (THE KEY TO THIS)

$$\frac{\text{Interest Rate}}{\text{365 or 360 Days}} \times \text{Balance Of That Day} = \text{Interest Amount Of That Day}$$

$$\frac{6\%}{365} \times \$100{,}000 = \$16.44$$

KWAK

Let's say you have a line of credit balance of $100,000 with a 6% interest rate. The math behind the average daily interest is this.

You take the interest rate divided by 365 days. (Some banks may use 360 days which is called the "Commercial Lending Year". This is true with certain lines of credit programs that have to do with businesses.)

Once you have that number (small number), you multiply that by the balance you have on your line of credit for THAT specific day.

If you want to follow along, you'll take 0.06 (which is 6% divided by 365) and multiply it by $100,000. The illustration above shows that today's average daily interest is $16.44.

Again, that's the interest that you pay for THAT day for the balance you have.

But what if the balance changes the next day? What if the balance decreases to say $95,000? Would that affect the interest amount?

It sure would!

<u>So, here's the pinnacle question for you...</u>

What if we can take our entire income and pay the balance on our line of credit, thus keeping the interest amount low WHILE still being able to use the income to pay OUR expenses?

I'm starting to hear the explosions in your head! :)

If you don't get it quite yet, don't worry. Here's another illustration:

Here's an Example...

	Day 1	Day 2	Day3	Day 4	Day 5	Day 6	Day 7
Interest	$16.44	$15.62	$15.69	$15.75	$15.78	$15.81	$15.81
Balance	$100,000	$95,000	$95,500	$95,800	$96,000	$96,200	96,200
Income	$0	$5,000	$0	$0	$0	$0	$0
Expense	$0	$0	$500	$300	$200	$200	$0

In this illustration, we're showing you an example scenario of using this strategy for 6 days.

On Day 1, we start with the $100,000 line of credit balance with a 6% interest rate.

On Day 2, we deposit our income of $5,000 into the line of credit which brings down the line of credit balance to $95,000. If you notice, the interest that we are getting charged now is only $15.62 for that day. instead of $16.44

On Day 3, we have to spend some money, right? Let's say we went out and spent $500 out of our line of credit. This could be for groceries, gas, dining, etc.

Now, we have a new balance of $95,500 for that day which also means that we are getting charged $15.69 of interest for that day.

So, if we continue this pattern, we are only getting charged $110.90 of interest for the 7 days. Had we kept the balance at $100,000 at 6%, we would have paid $ 115.08.

Now, we know that doesn't seem like a big number but the effect of this tiny savings does have a long-term "compounding effect".

But we'll do you one better.

What if we kept the balance at $95,000 from Day 2 through Day 7, but pay for our expenses at no additional cost to our interest? Do we have your attention?

There's a method that we've discovered called the "Hybrid Method" which involves using a credit card. Now, we know some of you are not big fans of credit cards but hear us out.

Credit cards often give you 21-30 days of a grace period before the actual interest kicks in. So if you go buy groceries today with a credit card, you have until the next billing cycle where you pay zero interest on the purchase.

What if we can use our credit cards to pay for all of our living expenses and pay it off before the end of the billing cycle? Wouldn't that mean that we've gotten away with paying zero interest on our credit card?

What's even better is that if you have a credit card that gives you points or cash back rewards, you now have earned some pretty neat perks! At the same time, you paid zero interest!

So if we couple this with the fact that we can leave our line of credit balance at $95,000 for an awfully long period of time, that means that we would only owe $110.16 instead of $115.08.

Again, that seems like a small number but if we zoomed out and saw another 7 days with the $95,000 balance. We would pay $219.50 of interest in the span of the 14 days.

But, if we kept the balance at $100,000 for the same 14 days, we would have paid $230.16. You can begin to see that the gap is getting wider and wider between what you would have paid versus what you are paying now.

You can't do this with a mortgage because you don't get to deposit your entire income into the mortgage and pay for your living expenses at the same time.

With the line of credit, it allows you to deposit your entire income towards the balance, use your credit card for the zero interest, and withdraw the funds out of the line of credit at the end of the credit card billing cycle to completely pay it off.

By doing this, the line of credit had a significant reduction on its balance for 21-30 days since you have not had to withdraw any funds out of the line of credit.

Pretty sweet, huh?

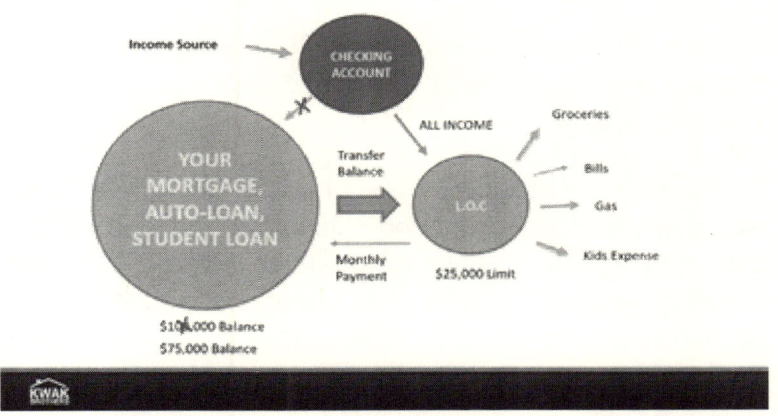

So, let's put it all together…

Here's ONE way of using this strategy. There are different variations of this strategy and it depends on your situation.

This is called the 2nd Lien Position Path – also known as the "chunking method".

In this example, we have a $25,000 limit on a line of credit. That could be a Home Equity Line of Credit (HELOC), a Personal Line of Credit (PLOC) or a Business Line of Credit (BLOC). Let's say your mortgage balance is $100,000.

Keep in mind, the $25,000 amount is something we can use up to. You don't have to use the entire $25,000.

What we're doing is taking that $25,000 line of credit and making a principal payment against the mortgage. Now, we have a balance of $25,000 on your line of credit. Your mortgage balance has been reduced to $75,000.

By doing this, you just saved THOUSANDS of dollars of interest on your mortgage which also means that you've saved time as well.

Next, we have to tackle the line of credit. Remember how taking your entire income and putting it in your HELOC lowers the average daily balance which lowers the interest amount? That's what we're doing here. But we still have to spend money on bills, groceries, and other life expenses, right?

You can still spend that money out of line of credit! Ideally, you want there to be sometime between your income deposit into the line of credit and when you spend the money out of it so that you can keep the average daily balance on the line of credit low.

In a perfect world, it would be ideal if you could deposit your income into the HELOC on the 1st day of the month and withdraw the funds needed for expenses on the 30th day.

This is so that you have 30 days of a "gap" where your line of credit balance was significantly reduced. In those 30 days, you were subjected to a reduced interest amount since the line of credit uses daily balance to calculate the interest. That's why the hybrid method is super effective.

Pretty clever, huh?

In other words, cash flow management allows you to change how interest is calculated down to the daily level. Small daily interest reductions grow exceptionally large over time. If we can reduce the balance today that means we won't be charged interest on that balance today, tomorrow, next week, next month or next year.

Our goal is to get the balance as low as possible as fast as possible and keep the balance as low as possible as long as possible. This is how you avoid interest.

1st Lien HELOC vs. a 2nd Lien HELOC.

Now, we've already mentioned these two different types of Home Equity Lines of Credit. But some of you may not be familiar with either or perhaps you don't understand the differences.

The traditional HELOC as many of you already know is the 2nd Lien HELOC. A 2nd lien HELOC is set up in a way where you keep your existing mortgage but you're getting another loan on top of it.

So let's say you own a $100,000 home at its current value. You still owe $50,000 on your primary mortgage. But because you have $50,000 of equity, the bank can give you $30,000 of that as a 2nd lien HELOC (80% LTV: Loan to Value).

Ultimately, you now have the $50,000 mortgage and a $30,000 HELOC limit. Keep in mind that you don't have to use the entire $30,000 limit.

On the flip side, a 1st lien HELOC is different. Instead of getting a HELOC on top of the existing mortgage, you're completely replacing the mortgage with a HELOC.

So back to our earlier example of a $100,000 home. You currently owe $50,000 and therefore you have $50,000 worth of equity. Instead of getting a HELOC on top of the existing mortgage, the bank will give you a HELOC to completely replace the mortgage. Therefore, the mortgage doesn't exist anymore. All you have now is just a HELOC and that's the only debt that is collateralizing your home.

There's pros and cons to each of the lien positions and it ultimately depends on your goals, risk tolerance, preference and what saves you more money at the end of the day.

Also, not all banks offer the 1st lien position HELOC. Most banks will offer the 2nd lien HELOC. This is why our clients come to seek our help to determine which lien position might be the best fit for them and where to even get the 1st lien HELOC.

Quick Note About Interest Rates

Let's quickly talk about interest rates and why you've been misled all of your life. "TIP" is the most important number in real estate finance. T.I.P. stands for Total Interest Percentage. It's the percentage you pay as a total compared to the amount you borrowed over the life of the loan.

You may have a $300,000 mortgage at 2.75% on a 30-year fixed amortized loan, but your TIP will still be 53%. This is disclosed[1] in the small print in a mortgage loan but is not discussed as the banks want you to focus on the 2.75% because it's the lowest number they can put in front of you. It's a complete misdirection. The banks want you to focus on the interest rate, not the TIP.

Most people know their interest rate but have no idea what their TIP is or even know what it means. We want to manage cash flow so we can significantly reduce our TIP. As an example, if you use a HELOC and borrow $300,000 at the same 2.75% rate with a .50% rate increase each year you can reduce your TIP from 53% down to 23%.

This assumes cash flow results in a 10-year payoff. This is even with the fact that the rate is adjustable and rising .50% each year. The simple interest of the HELOC and implementation of cash flow strategies has tremendous savings. The TIP is even lower if you pay off in less than 10 years.

Our goal is to help you lower the TIP so this saved interest can be reinvested. Interest is paid with a net dollar that has been taxed, you must fight for that net dollar. To avoid paying interest is a guaranteed return. Interest earned is taxable -- avoid interest first and earn interest second.

Interest rates are not the enemy in a HELOC! Balance and time are the enemy!

Therefore, the interest rates really don't matter in the context of this strategy. We can't believe how many people are so fixated on the interest rates but they fail to understand the bigger picture of the TIP.

Ch 4. What If?

So at this point you're thinking, "Wow! This is surprisingly good! But we have a ton of questions..." By now, some of you are 100% bought into the strategy. But for many of you, you still have concerns and doubts.

That's totally okay! We had the same questions and doubts when we first learned about this strategy many years ago.

So, let's tackle some of the more common questions we get all the time.

"WHY CAN'T I JUST PUT EXTRA PAYMENTS INTO THE MORTGAGE?!"

Ah, we get this one all the time! It's probably the most obvious question, right? You're thinking, "Why do we have to go through this HELOC thing?! Why can't we stick to the traditional method of paying extra directly into the mortgage?"

And you're not alone in asking that question!

We would like for you to meet Ed! Ed is one of our clients and he was doubtful of the strategy as well! He was a "never-HELOC" person. He didn't quite understand the benefits and the advantage that the Accelerated Banking Strategy has. But after listening to us "preaching the good news" about the strategy, he became convinced. Here's what he has to say now:

From Notifications

We used to pay off about 200 dollars principle monthly, with our new HELOC it looks like this..

CREDIT CHANGES

Balance Decreased by $4,446

Between July 31, 2019 and August 31, 2019, your account balance decreased by **$4,446** from $134,459 to $130,013.

So, Ed used to send $200 extra mortgage payment just towards the principal of his mortgage balance. That's the traditional way.

But after using our strategy, he paid down $4,446 in just 1 month! (wow!)

So, what made him change his mind? What made him go from a "HELOC atheist" to a "Faithful Accelerated Banking Follower"?

Three reasons.

#1 Reason – Liquidity Lock Up

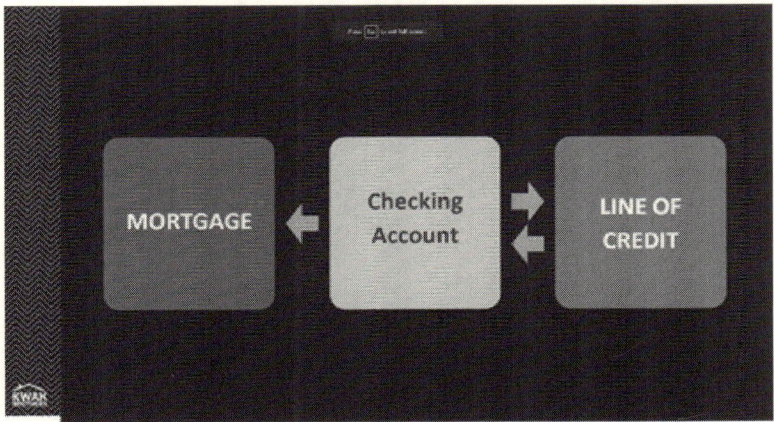

With a traditional mortgage, you're sure able to make extra payments directly to the principal balance. we will say that this does save money and time. But you lose something more critical to the modern economic needs.

Once you make an extra payment to the mortgage, you can't get any of that extra money back.

What happens if you need that extra cash for emergencies or an investment opportunity with a limited time offer?

At least with a line of credit, you're able to throw all kinds of extra money into the balance but you can still withdraw the funds for emergencies or for investments.

This makes a line of credit very flexible and gives you options.

In fact, we had several clients who decided to buy cars in the middle of using the strategy but still experienced great results!

Reason #2 – Savings Account Vs. HELOC

But we can also hear you saying, *"But that's what a savings account is for! I already have 6-9 months of money saved up like my favorite radio talk show host told me to do!"*

Well, that's great until we ask you this question.

How much is your savings account paying you each year? Let alone, if you have any money sitting around in your checking account, how much is your checking account paying you?

Close to zero.

If you're one of those lucky individuals, you may be getting 1% APY on your savings account, right?

So let's say you have $10,000 saved up in your savings account earning you 1% APY each year. That's $100 a year.

At the time of us writing this book, inflation is around 2%. Basically, you're losing $100 a year by letting your money sit inside of your "savings" account. It's more like an "erosion" account because your money is doing nothing to benefit you.

The only benefactor of your savings account is the bank. They can take your deposit and borrow money from the Federal Reserve to be able to make more money. By the way, your local banks are borrowing money from the Federal Reserves using a line of credit. Coincidence? we think not.

So why are you letting your money sit in an erosion account?!

Instead, why not take that $10,000 and deposit it against the HELOC which can now help you save 2.5% to 5% each year. Even at the bottom end of that range, you could be saving $250 a year with certain HELOCs.

Best of all, you still have access to that $10,000 from your HELOC at any time!

When you compare the features of the HELOC and your savings account, there are no real differences as far as being able to draw money out.

With a HELOC, you can often login to your banking app and transfer funds into your checking account in a matter of seconds.

So let me ask you one more time.

Why are you still using a checking or a savings account?

Is it because that's the right thing to do?

And who said it was the right thing? Tradition? The banks?

If you start to question your financial thinking and why you do the things that you do, you'll start to understand that everything is designed to benefit the banks. Not you.

So it's time to start thinking differently about banking.

Reason #3 – Double Income Utilization

And lastly, remember how you can take your entire income and deposit it against the HELOC balance? Instead of making small extra payments, why not let your entire income do the work for you?

The same income that is affecting the average daily balance on the line of credit can also be used to pay for your expenses.

It's kind of like being able to use your income twice! Some call it "recycled money"!

"But what if the banks shut down my HELOC? Like they did in 2008-2012?"

This is another question we get quite often. Many of you have witnessed or experienced the nightmares of our great recession that occurred between 2008-2012.

Our opinion is that the recession actually started in 2005 – 2007. The reason why we believe this is that the banks were creating false systems and checks that loosened the lending standards. It became apparent to many economists and investors that the borrowers were getting extremely risky loans but the banks didn't care. They needed to feed the Wall Street Systems with more loans so that the banks could make more money.

One of the big contributors to the HELOCs getting shut down was over-leveraging. In order for banks to create more loans, they needed to create more demand and allow homebuyers to get access to money.

What the banks did was to create mortgages at 80% LTV (Loan-To-Value). For example, if a house was worth $100,000 then the banks were willing to lend at 80% LTV. What the banks were really saying is that they were willing to lend 80% of the $100,000 value of the home which is $80,000. The borrowers were expected to come up with the remaining down payment of $20,000.

However, what the banks did were to offer another loan for the down payment so that homebuyers didn't have to come up with money. Banks were trying to create $0 down situations to borrowers that didn't have the best finances and credit scores.

Oftentimes, these loans to cover the down payments were in the forms of a HELOC or a 2nd mortgage.

When the "music" stopped in March of 2008, home values started to fall like a rock. The same $100,000 home was now worth $70,000 as the artificial demand dried up. All of a sudden, these homeowners found themselves with a higher interest rate and no income.

As you can imagine, the banks started shutting down HELOCs left and right. These HELOCs had no assets to collateralize.

The bottom line was that homeowners who lost their HELOCs had too much debt. They had been using these HELOCs to go on vacations, purchase cars, and use it as a down payment for another property. It was basically a house of cards on the cusp of collapse.

In our strategy, our focus is to pay down the debt. It's not to incur or create more debt. It's to go from being a risky borrower to a less risky borrower.

In fact, out of the thousands of clients we have currently, we've yet to see a single person lose their HELOC. None of our clients had their HELOCs frozen, shutdown, or curtailed even through the COVID-19 pandemic.

Of course, there are other reasons as to why the banks will shut down a HELOC. For instance, if the homeowner engages in an illegal activity on their property, the bank has every right to shut down the HELOC and call it due right away.

I'm willing to bet that none of you will do anything illegal.

"So, what happens if there's a recession then?"

This is related to the last question about HELOCs getting frozen or shut down. What if there's a repeat of the 2008 recession? Or at very least, another COVID-19 Pandemic?

Fortunately, the Accelerated Banking Strategy can also act as a "safety net" in those situations.

We sincerely hope that none of you reading this will lose your jobs or income. But it can happen to any of us.

Let's say our economy goes back to a recession again. If your income goes down, you lose your job, or your business suffers – here's how the Accelerated Banking Strategy can help you stay afloat!

Remember how you can withdraw money from the HELOC at any time? In a situation where you lose your income or it goes down, you still need to cover your expenses, right? What you can do is take money out of the HELOC to not only cover for your everyday expenses, but you can use the same funds to also cover the minimum payment on the HELOC itself.

This is called "floating" the debt. You're essentially using the debt to pay for its own minimum payments.

Now, is this meant to be a permanent solution? No.

But, is it meant for you to use the HELOC to stay afloat for 6-9 months until you can get back on your feet? Yes.

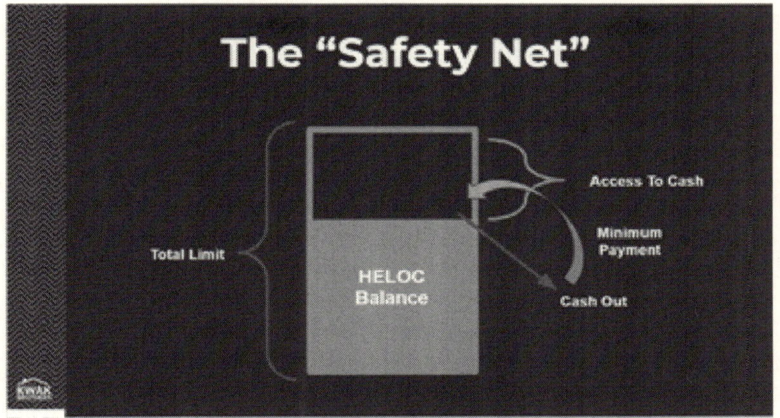

Using the HELOC will increase your debt balance temporarily but what are the alternatives? Not pay your bills? In the worst-case scenario, the alternative can lead you to a foreclosure situation or having late payments reported on your credit report.

Both of those hypothetical situations have long-term repercussions and consequences.

Having a HELOC at least allows you to avoid that.

You see, the strategy can act as a "lifeboat" for a couple of months until you can recover.

In fact, we had a client who unfortunately lost her job for 2-3 months during the COVID-19 pandemic. Initially, she panicked but then she remembered this very explanation we had given to her. She was already using the strategy at the time so she had a HELOC ready to go.

She was able to cover all her expenses and bills during the 2-3 months when she was furloughed. She survived the pandemic unscathed. Yes, her HELOC balance did increase but it only set her back a few more months in terms of her savings. Nevertheless, she was able to stay on track to beat the traditional timeframe of paying off her mortgage.

"But, I don't have enough equity to get a HELOC!"

Now, some of you reading this might have this problem. Maybe you bought your home with an FHA loan or a VA (Veterans Affair) loan just like Rick:

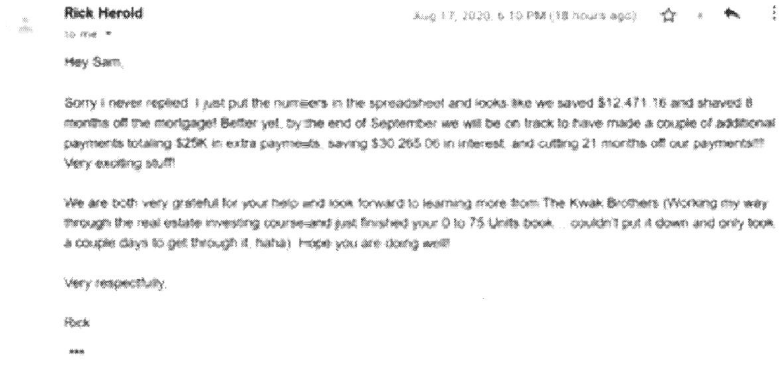

Rick Herold
to me

Aug 17, 2020, 6:10 PM (18 hours ago)

Hey Sam,

Sorry I never replied. I just put the numbers in the spreadsheet and looks like we saved $12,471.16 and shaved 8 months off the mortgage! Better yet, by the end of September we will be on track to have made a couple of additional payments totaling $25K in extra payments, saving $30,265.06 in interest, and cutting 21 months off our payments!!! Very exciting stuff!

We are both very grateful for your help and look forward to learning more from The Kwak Brothers (Working my way through the real estate investing course and just finished your 0 to 75 Units book... couldn't put it down and only took a couple days to get through it, haha). Hope you are doing well!

Very respectfully,

Rick

Rick was a Navy doctor in southern California and he wanted to use our strategy to pay down his mortgage. But he was hesitant to jump in because he believed that it was impossible to get a HELOC since he had no equity.

When he bought his home, his VA loan program allowed him to do zero money down. Therefore, he had no equity on his property.

Fortunately, there was an alternative vehicle for Rick. Instead of using a HELOC where it would typically require at least 10% equity, we were able to help Rick get a PLOC (Personal Line of Credit).

A PLOC works just like a HELOC. The only difference is that a PLOC doesn't use your home equity as a collateral. It's an unsecured non-recourse line of credit. Some of you familiar with this strategy already may think that Rick could have just used a credit card.

The problem with using a credit card as a vehicle is that credit cards are not as liquid as a true line of credit. In other words, it's often expensive to get cash out of a credit card. There are cash advance fees or sometimes transactional fees of up to 2.9% every time. Therefore, we're not big fans of using a credit card for the Accelerated Banking Strategy.

After using our strategy for just 2 months, Rick was able to save close to $42,000 on his mortgage interest and shaved

29 months off of his mortgage amortization schedule! (WOW!) And remember, that's without any equity at all!

So if you're in a similar situation to Rick, there is a way!

"What if I have a 15-year mortgage" or "Why don't I just get a 15-year mortgage?!"

Even with a 15-year mortgage, you can still use our strategy and get great results like Tom:

Joined in October and after researching the various options of the program, we applied for a HELOC through our local credit union. We have a 15 year mortgage and are 2.2 years into it. The program works even with a 15 year mortgage!! After applying the chunking hybrid method for just one month, the outstanding balance we currently have wouldn't have been reached until October 2021!!! The keys are discipline and a positive cash flow.

Tom has a 15-year mortgage and he's 2.2 years into it. He shared his story with me back in October 2019. After using our strategy for just 1 month, he saved 2 years!

In this case, Tom used a 2nd lien position HELOC to do our Accelerated Banking Strategy. He did a single chunk payment on his 15-year mortgage and that was his result.

Also keep in mind that our clients are taught to subtract any interest or time spent on paying down the HELOC as well to get the true "net results".

"But I live paycheck to paycheck... Can this strategy still work?"

Ideally, you'll want to have a positive cash flow situation. In other words, your expenses must be less than your income amount. It's reported that 63% of the average Americans live paycheck-to-paycheck (3).

However, it's one thing if you're actually living paycheck-to-paycheck but it's another thing to simply spend whatever money you have in the bank. There's a clear difference.

The first type of "paycheck-to-paycheck" is you spending every dollar to necessary limits. Perhaps you're already budgeting.

The second type is you spending without actually tracking anything. You don't know whether you're actually living paycheck-to-paycheck because you never took the time to measure and track.

In some cases, people who begin to track their spending and intentionally stick to a plan find themselves with a positive cash flow after all. They stopped spending every dollar in their bank account without a plan.

Fortunately, if you're in the paycheck-to-paycheck mode, there are ways out of it

If having too much debt is the primary reason, one way to mitigate this is to consolidate the debt as much as possible.

One time, we had a situation where a client had over 15 credit cards. Each individual card did not have that big of a balance. It was a couple of hundred dollars due here and there.

What we suggested was to roll all the card balances into a single credit card where it'd be more manageable and also decrease the monthly payment obligation! Instantly, they weren't living paycheck-to-paycheck anymore.

From there, this client was able to use our strategy to ultimately pay off the credit cards and focus on paying off their mortgage.

"But I have inconsistent income! How does this strategy work for me?"

If you own a business or you get paid commissions, your income might be inconsistent. We have many real estate agents as clients and this is the number one question we get from them!

Fortunately, this strategy can also work well even if you have an inconsistent income.

Meet Martha!

Martha and her husband own a highly successful construction company. Most construction companies have seasons. During winter months, it slows down. During summer months, it gets busy!

Martha had the same concern before getting started in our strategy. But after explaining how this strategy works even with the inconsistency, she went to work.

After 1 year of using our strategy, Martha paid off $107,733.70 of her mortgage principal!

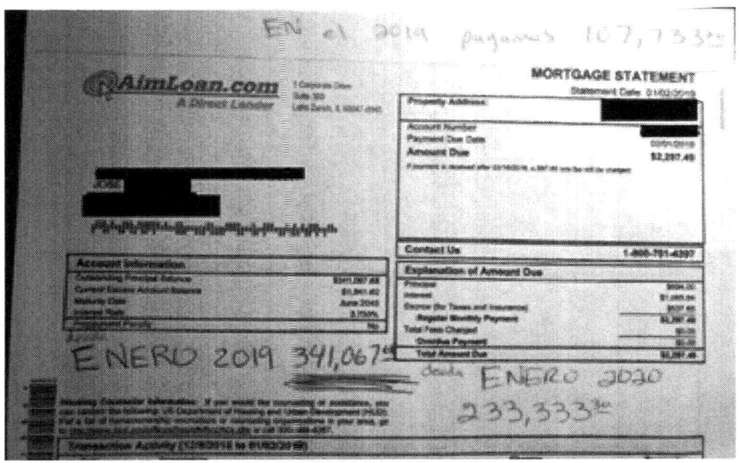
EN el 2019 pagamos 107,733

AimLoan.com
A Direct Lender

MORTGAGE STATEMENT

Contact Us

Explanation of Amount Due

Account Information

ENERO 2019 341,067

ENERO 2020 233,333

So how does this strategy work with inconsistent income? It's actually quite simple.

You first have to track a consistent expense budget every month. You get to know your number. Let's say your monthly living expenses come up to be $5,000.

Let's say in one particular month, you've earned $10,000. Just like what the strategy suggests, you'd deposit the entire $10,000 directly into the HELOC balance. (You can always use the hybrid method to put most of your expenses on the credit card. This allows for the most optimal savings.)

You'll then use the HELOC to cover the credit card balance and any other obligations – which should total $5000.

The remaining $5,000 of savings will stay in the HELOC to lower the average daily balance.

But let's say in the following month, you came short and only earned $3500. In this case, you can always tap into the HELOC to cover the $5,000 living expenses consistently.

While you may have a loss of $1,500, the average of the two months still allows you to experience a lowered average daily balance. Get it?

So, if you have a sudden increase of income or a bonus, leave that in your HELOC until you're ready to use it. While the money stays dormant, you can have it save you money on interest.

We also encourage you to set aside some funds for vacations and other fun activities. After all, vacations and travel are part of what makes us human! We do not advocate anyone to live on "rice and beans" unless it's a necessary step for the better.

"But I haven't bought a home yet! How can I get started?"

So you're not a homeowner yet. That's okay! You actually have a head start on this strategy. If you're planning to buy a home in the next 3-6 months, look into getting a 1st Lien Purchase HELOC instead of the traditional mortgage.

That is, instead of applying for a traditional 30-year mortgage, you can actually get pre-qualified for a purchase HELOC that can be used to finance the purchase of a home. This way, you don't have to get a mortgage first and then a HELOC. You can go straight into getting a HELOC.

The process is actually similar to the traditional method.

You'll contact one of the few banks that offer a 1st lien purchase HELOC and go through a pre-approval process. They'll check your credit and your income. The bank will then determine your pre-approved amount.

Using that pre-approved amount, you now have an idea of how much the bank is willing to fund your purchase. Most real estate agents we talk to prefer to work with home buyers that have a pre-approval letter anyway. So this is a necessary step before you go searching for your next home.

"But this sounds too good to be true!"

Ahh, the good ole "too good to be true" statement. Isn't anything new "too good to be true"?! We know this strategy is different, weird, or it may not make sense to you just yet.

Can you imagine how Galileo felt as he shared his discovery of the Earth's true shape?. Most people at his time thought that the Earth was flat. Some people, to this day, believe that it is!

When Galileo first told people about this newfound truth, the authorities at the time rejected it. It was weird, different, and didn't make sense to a lot of people.

Yet today, almost everyone knows that the Earth is actually a sphere.

To many of you, this strategy might rattle your traditional thinking and it may take some time for you to really understand it. And that's okay!

Many of our clients felt the same before they started using our strategy. But after going through the process, our clients are amazed at the results. Just take a look at our track record:

Yes, we're an accredited business with the Better Business Bureau. At the time of this writing, we are rated "Excellent" on Trustpilot with flawless 5-star reviews on Google. We definitely intend to keep it that way with more happy clients.

Of course, we've gotten the attention of the press as well. *Money Magazine* first reached out to us to interview us. Then, we were featured on NBC, Fox News, *MarketWatch*, and more.

If this strategy didn't work, we certainly wouldn't have garnered the attention of the media. We certainly wouldn't have received 5-star reviews on our independent rating platforms.

Ch.5 What Comes After The Strategy

So, we talked about paying off your mortgage using the Accelerated Banking Strategy. Awesome! But… we don't want to stop there. Now that we stopped your financial "bleeding", we want to start growing your financial "muscle".

If you are not interested in making more money, working less, and retiring early -- you can skip this chapter.

For the rest of you, the first thing you can do after the strategy is investing in real estate.

We know some of you have zero interest in this but hear this out. Once you are mortgage-free and you're armed with a line of credit, you now have some "EXPLOSIVE" tools in hand to start creating passive income.

Passive income is income that you don't have to actively work for. Just imagine as you sit back and relax. On the 1st of every month, you open your mailbox and you see envelopes filled with rent checks and they are written out to you!

Since we live in a digital age, all you have to do is login to your online banking site and see all the online payments that came in. While you're on a vacation, enjoying your freedom and the time with your family, your tenants are busy at work.

They are fighting traffic, dealing with the work politics, and putting in 50-70 hours a week just so that they can write the most important check: their rent payment!

It's kind of like being the queen bee. You've got your worker bees that fly out there to collect nectar from flowers. Then they fly back to your nest so that they can make you honey.

So, let's say that you've paid off your mortgage completely. And let's also say that you have a 1st Lien Home Equity Line of Credit that's also free and clear. In this scenario, you have a $300,000 line of credit that you can access for pretty much anything!

One of the things that we teach is the ability to buy houses and apartment buildings using owner financing.

Owner financing is a concept where you negotiate an arrangement with a seller of a property to make monthly financing payments to the seller as if they are the bank.

So instead of going to the bank to get a loan for a house, you can arrange a banking relationship with your seller.

If you can find the right property and the numbers support the fact that it has some great cash flow potential, you can buy the property with owner financing, and use your line of credit to make the down payment and cover the cost for repairs.

Many times, you can negotiate for extremely low-down payments. we'll share an example through a case study later.

The assumption here is that the rent you're collecting also covers taxes, insurance, management fees, ongoing maintenance, and improvements on the property.

Now that we're armed with this knowledge of Accelerated Banking Strategy, we can start paying off the line of credit like we did with the original mortgage we started off with.

Not only that, but you can also use the strategy on the owner financing arrangement so you can pay off the seller early.

Imagine repeating this process over and over to where you have 10 fully paid-off houses that generate $1,000 of cash flow to you each month? That's $10,000 a month of cash flow you're generating because you've been able to pay off your mortgages the same way we talked about earlier in this book!

Also, is it possible that we can buy multiple properties at once instead of waiting for the one house to be paid off?

Absolutely!

So, depending on your situation and your circumstances, your journey may look different.

Again, it's not about how you start but it's about how you finish!

If you can generate an additional $10,000 a month in cash flow, will that make a difference in your life?

Some of you may choose to retire early.

Maybe it can supplement your current income or your job.

Maybe you can take more frequent vacations and explore around the world.

Or maybe you can help your parents retire.

Whatever it means to you, it can make a world of difference in helping you have security and freedom.

You may be saying, *"But don't I have to manage the houses and the tenants? What if the toilets break or something goes wrong?!"*

We won't lie to you by saying that everything will be perfect with unicorns and rainbows. Sometimes bad things can happen.

One time we had to spend $3,000 to fix up a house because the tenants had left it completely trashed and destroyed. However, if you set aside a reserve for maintenance expenses, you'll be covered.

What you also want to have is **a professional property manager** to handle the daily operations. Instead of YOU taking all the phone calls and emails, you can have a dedicated professional deal with the problems instead.

The bottom line is this Get educated and know what you're doing.

If you asked Sam to fly an airplane, it's like asking him to partake on a suicide mission because he doesn't know how to fly an airplane. It would not only put him at risk but put others in the plane at risk.

But if he goes through classes and learns how, he may just well be able to fly the plane.

It's all about knowledge. In anything, you reduce your risk of facing bad things if you have the knowledge to prevent bad things from happening. And when the bad things do happen, you'll have the knowledge to respond quickly without costing you a whole lot.

It's like driving. At first, you were a huge risk driving on the road because you didn't know what you were doing. But after a series of lessons and supervised training, you got the hang of it. Soon, you were driving and texting at the same time as a pro! (Just kidding, don't do this… It's dangerous!)

In all seriousness, anything can be mastered. You just have to practice, learn, and hone in on the new skills of becoming a real estate investor.

Sam's Deal Case Study - $2500 Down for a $100 Monthly Cashflow

Let me share a perfect case study of a real life deal I did in 2017. It all began with emailing an attorney that represented an owner of a property in my area. I found this attorney through a software database called Propstream. By the way, you can get a free 7-day trial of Propstream here: http://reisoftware.thekwakbrothers.com

With Propstream, I was able to pull up a list of all the landlords in a specific area. What I did was look for specific landlords that had an LLC (Limited Liability Company) in which[2] they held their rental properties. I did this very strategically as I knew landlords with an LLC were probably serious and they most likely have multiple properties. The chance of them selling a property is pretty high.

I probably sent out close to 25 emails to different attorneys and landlords at the time, asking if they would be interested in selling any of their properties. One replied back saying that he would be interested in selling a single-family home. Bingo!

The seller and I met at the property and conducted a thorough walk through to make sure that the property didn't have massive problems. Massive problems can be a nightmare.

The seller was asking for $90,000 for the single-family home. The rent rate at the time was $1200 a month. With a little bit of quick math, I knew this could be a deal to be made.

Here's the best part: I was able to negotiate with the seller to agree on owner financing. They were willing to take monthly payments from me in exchange for the ownership rights of the property. Of course, the seller was also asking for a down payment. I offered $5,000 for the down payment. At the time, I had this money so I was prepared to close whenever.

With the help of my attorney, we got a contract drafted and we were ready to sign. But here's another best part: I also negotiated for one month's rent and the security deposit as a closing credit against my down payment. The total amount for the credit ended up being $2500.

So that $2,500 closing credit was subtracted from my down payment which cut my down payment in half. I only had to bring $2,500 cash to the closing table to get this closed.

This property cashflows around $100 a month and I've built over $50,000 of equity in just 2 years. This was a MAJOR win for me. When I combine my equity gain through appreciation and my cashflow, my return on investment was 1,400%. Talk about a great deal.

So imagine having a HELOC or a line of credit to do this over and over again!

Keep in mind, by using owner financing, I didn't have to get a bank loan which meant that I didn't have to use my credit. Since the owner financing payments don't appear on my credit report, it doesn't affect my debt-to-income ratio. This means that I could go get a bank loan if I really needed to get a deal done.

My brother and I got so good at doing this that we developed a system called the FORCE strategy. It stands for:

1. Find the Deal.
2. Owner Finance It
3. Raise the Capital.
4. Cashflow It
5. Expand Your Empire!

It was the perfect system for massive growth within a very short amount of time.

Don't get me wrong. It takes time and patience through getting educated to pull off something like this. It didn't happen to us overnight. We spent nearly three years perfecting our craft before we got to this point.

But here's the best part, if you leverage the success of other people and get them to help you, the success can come quicker than figuring things out on your own.

Becoming Your Own Bank

We've had many of our clients also transition into becoming their own bank. After 2-3 months of using our strategy, they start to see all kinds of possibilities – not just real estate investing.

About three years ago, we discovered a concept and a strategy that allows an individual to become their own bank. Sounds interesting, right?

It's called the Infinite Banking Concept, or IBC for short. This concept has been around for almost 150 years and is used by some of the wealthiest families. (It's been said that the Rockefeller family uses this method to retain their wealth and pass down their generational wealth.)

So if you combine the Accelerated Banking Strategy together with IBC, it allows you to completely break free from the mainstream banking system.

Here's how it works.

The Infinite Banking Concept relies on using a whole life insurance policy that allows you to overfund your cash value.

There's a lot of misinformation out there about using other forms of life insurance policies. But after a long search for the truth, we've discovered that it has to be a whole life policy. And not just any whole life policy, it has to be a very specific policy where you can borrow against your cash value as a non-direct recognition loan. We'll talk more about this later.

Once you acquired this specific whole life insurance policy, you'll begin to make your premium payments to start building up your cash value.

Let's say over time, you built a cash value of $100,000. The cool part about the $100,000 cash value is that the insurance company is paying you dividends on it. So, if the insurance company is paying you a 5% dividend yield each year, that means, your cash value is growing by 5% each year.

Here's the better part. You can take out a loan against the $100,000 as a collateral to buy real estate, fund your child's education, or buy a business. You get to decide how much interest you pay on the loan and when to pay it off. This is possible because the insurance company has a private contract with you.

So let's say you borrow $50,000 against the $100,000 cash value. With the right whole life policy, you can still earn the 5% dividend yield on the entire $100,000 cash value even though you just borrowed $50,000.

One of our good friends often borrows from his cash value to fund his next real estate deal. In his situation, he gets to profit three times. The first from his real estate deal, the second from the interest he's paying himself directly into the cash value, and the third is coming from the cash value dividends.

Holy smokes! Talk about triple growth opportunities. Can you see how using this strategy paired with accelerated banking and real estate investing, you can have rocket growth?!

Now it's really important that you have a whole life policy where it allows for a non-direct recognition loan because this allows you to earn a dividend on the entire cash value even if you borrowed all of it.

As a contrast, if you use a direct recognition loan, borrowing against the cash value means that your cash value is earning less dividend since they subtract the loan amount from the cash value as the amount subject to dividends.

There's a lot more to this infinite banking strategy and you can find an entire book on this concept. I just want to paint the possibility as to how Accelerated Banking Strategy fits into all this.

The possibility we want to help you create is a personal ecosystem. We want you to build a financial ecosystem where everything you do is growing your wealth.

Imagine taking a vacation by borrowing from your cash value and paying yourself the interest. All while your cash value is still growing.

Imagine buying a car and financing it out of your cash value instead of feeding the interest to the banks. You can now put more cash into your own pocket – not the banks.

Think of it like this. The Accelerated Banking Strategy is like planting the seed in the soil. Real estate investing is like the fertilizer to help the plant grow. And the Infinite Banking Concept is like taking seeds that the fruit produces to go plant more seeds.

Can you see how powerful the three strategies can become when you combine them?

Ch 6. How To Get Started

Okay, so here it is! Let's talk about how to actually start using this strategy to save money. But the #1 question we get all the time about getting started is: *"This strategy sounds like it's too hard or it takes too much discipline!"*

We totally get that. In fact, the team has dedicated our last five years to turning this strategy into an automated system. We're never done perfecting it but we've built a system where any qualified homeowner can easily use our strategy.

We've learned in the early days of this business that no matter how awesome something is, no one is going to use it if it's too complicated.

With the help of industry professionals and experts, we turned our Accelerated Banking System into an automated process where all you have to do is virtually "flip a switch" and you're using the strategy.

Best of all, we also developed a relationship with banks that will run everything in the background for you so that you don't have to worry about the steps.

Now of course, many of you might also say, *"I can figure this out on my own! I can just Google all the answers and the steps on how to do it!"*

It's true. You can probably spend the time figuring this out on your own. And yes, there are free resources out there that you can probably tap into. But consider this: If there's free information out there on YouTube and Google on how to become a millionaire, why isn't everyone a millionaire? How come even with the free resources on the internet, we still have people struggling financially.

Early in our entrepreneurial career, we had a huge epiphany. If you're not surrounded by people who are actively using the Accelerated Banking Strategy, then you won't. Well, what do We mean by that?

It's called the law of association. If five of your closest friends are drug addicts with no vision, no goals, and no financial stability, it's likely that you'll also become a drug addict with no vision, no goals, and no financial stability.

On the flip side, if the five of your closest friends are building investments with visions, goals, and a purpose, it's also likely that you'll catch on to building investments as well.

So, it's all about who is in your nearest influence. We always believe that if we can surround ourselves with people who are experts and are a lot smarter than we are, then we will be motivated to become experts as well.

Another way to look at this is that if you want something done, rather than trying to figure it out, you can pay an expert to help you do it. Then your focus is doing what you are great at and keep on improving it.

For instance, say you're not the best at repairing a roof. So instead of "trying to save a few bucks" by doing it on your own, you let the experts do it. Not only will the job get done correctly, but you can also keep your focus on your business and investments where you know you can make more money.

It's all about proper allocation of time and priority.

So, here's the deal.

You can choose to do this on your own, spend all your time and energy figuring this out. But, we must warn you, we've had countless individuals who chose this route and ultimately ended up coming back to the team for help. In fact, they were in a worse situation than they were in before they got started

The most common mistakes we see are that people get the wrong kind of a HELOC, or they do the steps incorrectly, or they get burned by the wrong mortgage broker and get a home equity LOAN instead. There are all kinds of mistakes that we see people make when trying to do this on their own.

Sometimes, they have to spend money to get out of the hole they dug themselves into. What a waste!

The alternative option (the smart plan) is to let experts like our team set everything up for you. Not only will you potentially save more money, but it also saves the emotional stress and headaches.

Our team has over 70+ years of experience in banking, finance, credit, and the mortgage industry to understand the process.

It's kind of like using a GPS in your own neighborhood. When you first move to a new town or a city, you'll probably use a navigation app to help you get around, right? But after a while, you don't need the navigation or the GPS anymore because you begin to rely on your memory and habits.

Well, our team has seen thousands of different situations across the country to know how this strategy works and doesn't work. This strategy is like our neighborhood and we've been here for a while.

But for someone new like you, you may need a GPS or a navigation app to help you get around. In this analogy, we are the "GPS" where we can give you the turn-by-turn direction.

Sometimes, you may make the wrong turn and we'll have to "re-calculate" you to a different route.

So here's the next step.

If you want our expert help, all you have to do is schedule a FREE 45 Minute call with our team to discuss the next steps. In this free call, we're going to discuss four main things:

1. Should you and can you do this strategy?
2. How much money and time can you potentially save? (We'll even get you an estimated pay-off date.)
3. Answer any personal questions you may have about your situation.

4. How our process works in terms of becoming a client.

To schedule a call, use this link:
https://acceleratedbanking.com/consulting

Now, we know what your next question is.

"How much is it to work with you and your team?"

Can't you tell that Sam is secretly a mind reader? Just kidding!

Here's the cool part. If you don't end up saving money and time with our help, you don't pay anything. That's right. If you apply what we teach you to do and if you don't see your mortgage balance decrease faster than the traditional method, then you don't pay anything. There's zero cost!

And here's the next cool part. If you apply for a line of credit and get denied three times, you also don't pay anything.

Now, those are rare situations because our team is great at making sure you're a good fit or not. So let's say you save a ton of money and time, you're extremely happy, and we're able to help you get closer to your goal. All we're asking is for a tiny fraction of what you'll save as the initial investment to get started. That's it!

So wait, where's the cost then? There is no cost. You'll only save money because what you'll save through this strategy will overshadow any monetary investments you'll make to get the most optimized result.

How cool is that?

To schedule a call, use this link:
https://acceleratedbanking.com/consulting

Not only will we be part of your Accelerated Banking journey, but we also want to help you transition into real estate investing and also Infinite Banking which is something we talked about in the last chapter.

Schedule your FREE

45 Minute Discovery Call Today!

To schedule a call, use this link:

https://acceleratedbanking.com/consulting

- Find Out how much Time & Money You can potentially save using our method.
- Get answers to your unique questions about your unique situations
- Find out how you can work with the Accelerated Banking team virtually increase your success
- If we can't help you save money and time, you don't pay

Testimonials & Praises for Accelerated Banking

Arlene Pete ▶ Accelerated Banking Mastermind

2m ·

I got my 1st lien HELOC with [redacted] in March 2020 and made my last payment today. House is paid off! I was skeptical at first, but it really works!

Sam Kwak — 2 Comments

Accelerated Banking Mastermind

Group post by Maribeth Flores Patanao · 1h ·

2months update on 1st lien Heloc on March 2nd with $304,200 , today it's down to $280,800! We are so excited what our future hold , what a financial freedom ! Thanks Sam Kwak!

10 Comments

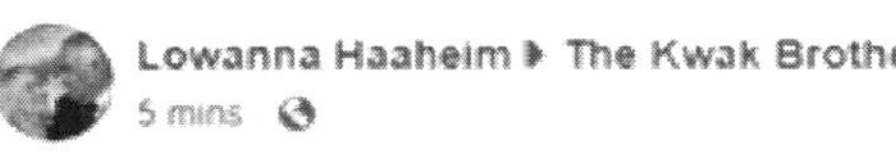
Lowanna Haaheim ▸ The Kwak Brothers
5 mins

Hi Sam, We just made our first 20 g mortgage chunk payment and saved $13,619.84 and 2.58 years of payments according to the amortization calculator! Thanks to your course, encouragement, videos, zoom meetings, and your personal input! Good job!!

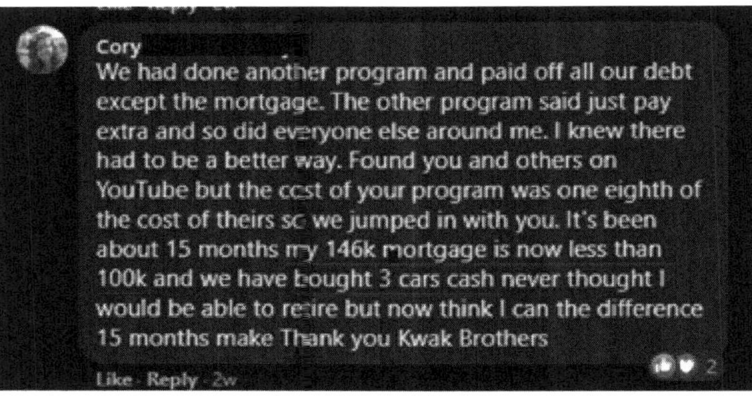
Cory

We had done another program and paid off all our debt except the mortgage. The other program said just pay extra and so did everyone else around me. I knew there had to be a better way. Found you and others on YouTube but the cost of your program was one eighth of the cost of theirs so we jumped in with you. It's been about 15 months my 146k mortgage is now less than 100k and we have bought 3 cars cash never thought I would be able to retire but now think I can the difference 15 months make Thank you Kwak Brothers

Like · Reply · 2w

Manalogs - the manalo vlogs 2:14 PM (5 hours ago)  

to Sam

Great . So Far we've paid down 8400 in 2 months!! As for real estate my mom is inquiring in some land in Vegas. My sister and I were thinking of doing small Airbnb's on it

AB

A Bulick

1 review · US

Apr 3, 2021

Beach bound, thanks Kwak Brothers!!

We went to Mortgage college with the Kwaks! We've relocated for work multiple time so we are always in the infant stages of a mortgage, paying too much interest and not enough principal. Using the Kwak's methods and in less than eight months, we have saved a substantial amount of interest and our mortgage is close to being done. We are buying our dream retirement home at the beach! Highly recommend (if you are disciplined person and will follow the plan!)

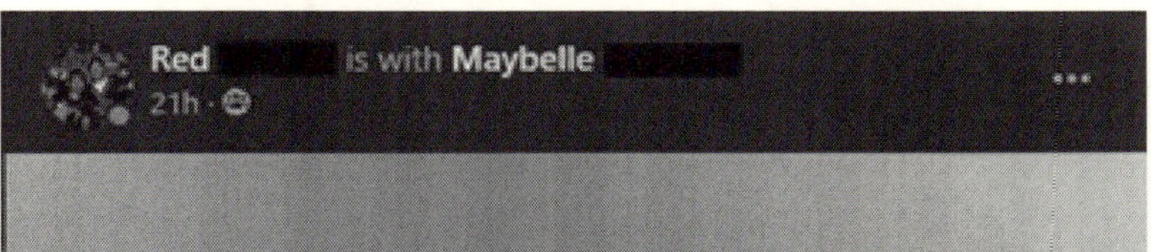

Started this journey back in November 2020 . We have paid off 31k as end of May!

Notes

(1) Slaughter, Patrick, October 3rd 2021. "5 Common Reasons Couples Divorce". https://www.jameslafevor.com/5-common-reasons-couples-divorce/

(2) U.S. Census Bureau, July 18th, 2020. https://www.census.gov/topics/population/migration/guidance/calculating-migration-expectancy.html

a. Long, Larry H. Migration and Residential Mobility in the United States. New York: Russell Sage Foundation, 1988, pp. 295-310.

b. Long, Larry H., and Celia G. Boertlein. The Geographical Mobility of Americans: An International Comparison. Washington, DC: U.S. Government Printing Office, 1976. Current Population Reports P23-64, pp 12-19.

(3) Leonhardt, Megan. December 11th 2020. "63% of Americans have been living paycheck to paycheck since Covid Hit" https://www.cnbc.com/2020/12/11/majority-of-americans-are-living-paycheck-to-paycheck-since-covid-hit.html

About The Authors

Sam Kwak is a serial entrepreneur, real estate investor, and a certified credit counselor. He has founded and launched multiple six and seven figure companies. He has a special talent in marketing, business development, finance, and technology. He and his brother, Daniel, currently manage a hedge fund company that invests in real estate.

David Bruce is a serial mortgage industry expert with nearly 30 years of experience. He is currently the Chief Operations Officer for Accelerated Banking. David has experience in working in the banking industry as well. With multiple perspectives on banking, mortgages, finance, and strategy, he has helped over thousands of homeowners get on track to becoming mortgage-free. As the user of Accelerated Banking Strategy himself, he was also able to pay off his own mortgage in just 13 months.